Talented
Active
Thoughtful
Easy going
Merciful

God made you special! He

will always be there for you.

♡ Mrs. Barrett

My First Prayers
for the Whole Year

Under the direction of Romain Lizé, Executive Vice President, MAGNIFICAT
Editor, MAGNIFICAT: Isabelle Galmiche
Editor, Ignatius: Vivian Dudro
Translator: Janet Chevrier
Proofreader: Claire Gilligan
Assistant to the Editor: Pascale van de Walle
Layout Designers: Élisabeth Hebert, Gauthier Delauné
Production: Thierry Dubus, Sabine Marioni

Maïte Roche

My First Prayers
for the Whole Year

MAGNIFICAT·Ignatius

Contents

Our Father

Our Father,
who art in heaven,
hallowed be thy name;
thy kingdom come,
thy will be done
on earth as it is in heaven.
Give us this day our daily bread,
and forgive us our trespasses,
as we forgive those who trespass against us;
and lead us not into temptation,
but deliver us from evil.

Amen.

Hail Mary

Hail Mary,

full of grace,

the Lord is with thee.

Blessed art thou among women

and blessed is the fruit of thy womb, Jesus.

Holy Mary, Mother of God,

pray for us sinners

now and at the hour of our death.

Amen.

My God, You Know Me by Name

My God,

you know me by name.

You love me like a daddy.

I am your child.

Help me to grow

closer to you every day.

Alleluia! Alleluia!

Amen.

Good Morning, Mary

Good morning, Mary!
Watch over me with love,
and open my heart
to welcome Jesus.
Help me to do what is right,
today and every day.

Amen.

Thank You, Lord

Thank you, Lord,
for this lovely day.
I pray to you
for my daddy and my mommy,
my family and my friends,
and everyone I met today.
I give you all my sorrows
and all my joys,
and I offer you
all the treasures of my heart.

Amen.

Good Night, Mary

Good night, Mary.

Into your care I entrust myself

and everyone I love.

Watch over us

with your motherly care,

keep us in God's love,

and help us sleep in peace

this night.

Amen.

Good Night, All You Holy Ones

Good night, Jesus.

Good night, Mary.

Good night, all you saints of God.

Good night, my guardian angel.

Watch over me

and over all those I love,

every night and every day.

Amen.

Jesus, I Love You

Jesus, I love you.
Come into my home,
and it will become your home.

Amen.

Jesus, My Friend

Jesus,

you are my friend.

When I am sad, comfort me;

when I am happy, share my joy;

when I go to sleep, watch over me.

Thank you, Jesus.

Amen.

Forgive Me, Jesus

Forgive me, Jesus,

for fighting, for getting angry, for not being nice.

Teach me how to be kind, to make peace,

and to love others as you love us.

Give me a brand new heart

so that I can bring peace and joy to others

the way you do.

Amen.

Thank You for My Family

Thank you, Lord, for my mommy's hugs.

Thank you for my daddy's smiles.

Thank you for my happy home.

Thank you for special meals.

Thank you for the joy of being together.

Thank you, Lord, for my family!

Amen.

A Gloria for Little Ones

Alleluia!

Glory to God, our Father,

for the life he gives us.

And for my baptism, alleluia!

For my godmother and godfather, alleluia!

For the great family of the children of God, alleluia!

Glory to God!

Amen.

Lord, Bless My Family

Lord, bless my family:
my mommy and my daddy,
and my grandmothers and grandfathers.
Lord, bless all the children,
from the youngest to the oldest:
brothers and sisters, cousins and friends.
Bless all the families of the world.
Keep our hearts as joyful
as on a wedding day.

Amen.

A Prayer
to the Holy Family

Jesus, Mary, and Joseph,

Holy Family of God,

pray for us.

Help us to serve one another,

and to do our little everyday tasks

with great love.

Amen.

A Magnificat for Little Ones

With you, Mary,

I say thank you for Jesus.

With you, Mary,

I sing out my joy:

"The Lord

does wonderful things for me.

Holy is his name!"

Amen.

A Nazareth Table Blessing

Lord, bless this meal
and those who prepared it.
Teach us to share the gifts you have given us,
like Jesus, Mary, and Joseph
around the table in Nazareth.

Amen.

A Sunday Prayer

Thank you, Jesus,
for Sunday!
You invite me to Mass.
Here I am.
I come to you
with my heart full of joy!
Alleluia! Alleluia!

Amen.

A Prayer
for Little Schoolchildren

My God,

bless my school

and all its teachers and students.

Give us the joy of learning.

Help us to work each day

to build together

your Kingdom of Love.

Amen.

A Prayer
to My Patron Saint

Saint ....,
the friend of God
whose name I bear,
guide me every day.
Patron saints of my family,
Saint .... and Saint ....,
protect us.
All saints in the family of God
who live in his light,
pray for us.

Amen.

42

Lord, Make Us Live in Love

Lord,

make us live and grow

in your Spirit of love.

Welcome close to you,

in the joy of your Kingdom,

all those who have left this life.

To you, who love us always,

I entrust my family and friends.

Amen.

Soon It Will Be Christmas!

Christmas is almost here!

Day after day,

I wait for you, Jesus,

and I prepare for your coming.

My house and my heart

are getting ready to welcome you.

Come, Jesus,

and light up our lives with your love.

Come, Lord Jesus!

Amen.

Christmas Is Here!

Christmas is here!

Glory to the newborn King!

Jesus, we come to you

to sing out our joy.

With your light guide our steps.

Glory to the newborn King!

Merry Christmas!

Amen.

With the Shepherds

Jesus, little Baby
lying in the manger
next to Mary and Joseph,
you look upon us and you love us.
With the shepherds
on Christmas night, Jesus,
I look upon you with wonder,
and I love you in return.

Amen.

Thank You
for Christmas Day

Thank you, Lord, for Christmas Day.

It's so good to be loved.

Thank you, Lord, for this day of joy.

It's so good to share

the happiness you give us.

Amen.

Here Come the Magi

Here come the Magi,
who followed the star.
They adore you, Jesus, and offer you
gold, frankincense, and myrrh.
You, the Lord, King of the Universe
and King of hearts,
you gather together
all the peoples of the earth
in the love of God,
our Father.

Amen.

A Prayer for Lent

Jesus,
open my hands to share
with my brothers and sisters.
Open my heart to forgive
and to make peace as you do.
Open my spirit to offer you my life.
Jesus, help me to live each day
in your love.

Amen.

Jesus,
You Who Carried the Cross

Jesus,

you who carried the cross,

teach me to love like you.

You who died to save us,

deliver us from evil.

You who offered yourself in love,

lead us to heaven.

You are our Savior!

Amen.

Alleluia! Jesus Is Alive!

Alleluia! Alleluia!

Easter is a day of joy!

Jesus, you are alive! You are risen!

You live within us

now and for ever.

Thank you, Jesus.

Alleluia! Alleluia!

Amen.

Jesus, Give Us Your Spirit

Jesus, give us your Spirit of love.

Help us to make peace with one another,

teach us to love one another as you love us,

and bring us together

in the joy of God,

our Father.

Amen.

Printed in June 2018 by Tien Wah Press, Malaysia
Job number MGN 18012
Printed in compliance with the Consumer Protection Safety Act, 2008